WONDERMENT

Ngozi Olivia Osuoha

TRANSCENDENT ZERO PRESS
HOUSTON, TEXAS

Copyright © 2019, Ngozi Olivia Osuoha.

PUBLISHED BY TRANSCENDENT ZERO PRESS
www.transcendentzeropress.org

All rights reserved. No part or parts of this book may be reproduced in any format whether electronic or in print except as brief portions used in reviews, without the expressed written consent of Ngozi Olivia Osuoha, or of the publisher.

ISBN-13: 978-1-946460-20-2
Library of Congress Control Number: 2019951332

Printed in the United States of America

Transcendent Zero Press
16429 El Camino Real Apt. #7
Houston, TX 77062

Cover image taken from
https://www.pinterest.com/pin/838373286866780671/?nic=1

Cover design by Glynn Monroe Irby

FIRST EDITION

WONDERMENT

Ngozi Olivia Osuoha

OTHER BOOKS BY NGOZI OLIVIA OSUOHA

THE TRANSFORMATION TRAIN
LETTER TO MY UNBORN
SENSATION
TROPICAL ESCAPE (Co-write)
FRUITS FROM THE POETRY PLANET
POETIC GRENADE
WHISPERS OF THE BIAFRAN SKELETON
CHAINS
FREEBORN
RAINDROPS
ECLIPSE OF TIDES
THE SUBTERFUGE
GREEN SNAKE ON A GREEN GRASS
CHARIOTS OF ARCHANGELS

DEDICATION

This poetry book is dedicated to the world.

Table of Contents

Wondering / 9
Doubts / 10
Wonders / 11
Trouble / 12
Mystery / 13
Division / 14
Vagabondage / 15
Legacy / 16
Still Wondering / 17
Fear / 18
Worried / 19
The Confusion / 20
Message / 21
Evil / 22
Payback / 23
Heartbreaking / 24
Foolishness / 25
Madness / 26
Craziness / 27
Greed / 28
Greediness / 29
Karma / 31
Pain / 32
I Need Answers / 33
Religious Madness / 34
Stigmatization / 35
Arrogance / 36
Ignorance / 37
Inequality / 38
Denial / 39
Gang / 40
The Secret / 41
Bleeding Heart / 42
Personal Interests / 43
Times / 44
Crooks / 45
Dowry / 46
Mourning / 47
Polygamous Family / 48

New School / 49
Jungle Justice / 50
Trespass / 51
Deceit / 52
Intruders / 53
Abuse / 54
Curiosity / 55
Tricks / 56
Society / 57
Hatred / 58
Change / 59
Fast Lane / 60
Behind the Scene / 61
Pampering / 63
Side Chicks / 64
Forgery / 65
Responsibilities / 66
Boundary / 67
Birds of the Same Feather / 68
Wonderment / 69
Purity / 70
BIO / 71

WONDERING

It bewilders me
How the world behaves
How pot calls kettle black,
And how the dead mock the living.

How immigrants tell history
History of aborigines,
How thieves boldly and loudly question
Questioning if they are thieves.

Tenants evict landlords
With powers, powers of money.

Prostitutes protest
Protesting against married women
Chasing them away,
Occupying their husbands.

How subjects dethrone kings
How slaves own their masters
How children parent and order their parents,
I am confused
I cannot fathom what's going on
How elders bathe at the market square
While children bathe in the womb.

DOUBTS

I have not come to terms
Terms with this present world
A world where everything is upside down.

Demons roam the street
Angels hide in heaven
Saints, down in grave
Godsends, gone and dead.

I have never believed all these
Though they happen daily
Daily, that I should be convinced,
Convinced beyond my powers.

Life is glaringly funny
At the same time, crazy
No one understands fully
None believes perfectly
Because, we live, we die, we quench
People at the same time, scarier than ghost.

WONDERS

It astonishes me
How the foetus beats the mother
For her to bend or break
How servants pride in poisoning,
And guards, in killing.

Yes, it does me marvel
Marvel, marvelous it is
How the kitchen starves the home
The home that houses it.

Fathers tell lies, dismantling their families
Mothers prefer certain children to others
Men marry wives, as many as possible
Legally, illegally, concubines and mistresses
Filling their house with different breeds
Breeds that cause confusion and commotion,
Commotions that scatter families
As families tear their ties.

TROUBLE

Relatives have become volcanoes
Volcanic eruptions, causing earthquakes
Earthquakes killing as many as possible
Destroying name, fame, pride, motto
Watchword, integrity, dignity, respect
Trust, sanity, sanctity and history.

They have turned devil, doing evil
Going about slandering, scandalizing
Gossiping, blackmailing, defaming
Disbanding, abusing, misusing and destroying reputations
Reputations built on solid rocks
Through ages, for ages, in ages and against ages.

These people are misfits
Vagabonds, prodigal sons, promiscuous rebels
Troublers, troubling hearts
Black sheep, and wayward fellows.

MYSTERY

It is still a wonder to me
How harlots crucify virgins
Virgins that are pure, innocent and blameless,
How they tangle and rope them in
Mesmerizing them with dirtiness.

It is hard to believe
Believe things that are invisible
Invisible things that never happened
It is unfortunate how they are cooked
Cooked, prepared, garnished and decorated,
That whoever sees, hears or knows about them
Starts believing, salivating, spreading them.

The world is cruel, yes very cruel
Cruel beyond doubts, beliefs, wars
Wars, that surpass human imagination
How do we cope with barbaric stories
Tragic events well organized, organized
Just to rubbish, tarnish and fracture people's image?

I still cannot assimilate how
How ants fight elephants
Elephants that are intimidating and gigantic.

DIVISION

It is a mystery how we cook division
How we boil and share segregation
How discrimination creeps in, into out bond
Bonds that have been ages
Ages intact, without any fault or pinch.

Pillars, strong pillars that have been through strikes
Quakes, lacks, wants, needs, sufferings and hardships.

These pillars emerge stronger and better
Alas storytellers twist them
Bend them, sidetrack them and crown themselves lords.

Innocent children born with purity unbound
Hope afloat, life and love unlimited
These ones derive hate from breast milk, water and food.
We have done more harm than good.

VAGABONDAGE

Cowards of little faith
Fools of small might
Illiterates of no wisdom
How they turn lions overnight
Lions roaring at hunters, tamers and shepherds,
But these lions fear the jungle.

Dwarfs of no bravery
Wayward beings of no discipline
Shouting at noble men
Flogging them with words and actions
Pouring our anger and frustrations
As though the noble made them lame.

Nobility is an ability
Bravery is a courage
The choice we make
The life we live
The outcome, the fate, the blessings
The curses, the cause and effect
We have little power of them.

Yes, it hurts me
It hurts me how reckless people outsmart
Outsmart men of valour.

LEGACY

The pages we write
The words we say
The actions we take
The dreams, hopes, aspirations and ambitions
These make or mar us.

We fool only men
We deceive only others
We manipulate ourselves
We shortchange humans
None can cheat God.

All things are temporary
All works shall be rewarded
All intents shall be tested
Whatever be they, however they are
We shall stand to reap them all.

STILL WONDERING

It frightens me, yes it does
How rogues play better
And the quiet lose worse
How touts live longer
And the reserved, otherwise
How mockers enjoy themselves
And the mocked, weep all day
All these really do frighten me.

It is a wonder, seriously it is
How jokers mean hell
And hell means lovers,
I fear it deep and deeper
How friends fight
And enemies, watch
How enemies guard, keep
And friends; waste, mourn.

This life is agonizing
It pierces my heart
It feeds my rage
How bones melt and flesh tear.

Honestly, I cannot understand
And people cause, enjoy and watch it happen,
I am still wondering.

FEAR

I fear the flock
The flock of women
That fight even wrongly
When their men are asleep.

I fear the flood
The flood of water
That washes away the land
The land for the future
And no one is talking,
They are busy, busy doing nothing.

It still angers me
Why people indulge in evil
Especially the evil that would wipe family
Kindred, community and clan.

They know not tomorrow counts
They do things against the godly
They trample themselves in ungodliness
Digging graves for innocent people
I fear their end.

WORRIED

How it irritates me
When guilty people prove sainthood
They always present themselves righteous
Accusing the righteous instead
O how I look and mourn
Yes, I mourn these ones
The ones that think silence is weakness.

I shake my head in pity
I pity them because they are foolish
Stupid crowd joining forces together
Coming against God, as if they can win.

They gang up among themselves
They tell terrible stories to humilate
They sidetrack, waylay, ambush, scatter
They do numerous horrors to be seen
To be heard, loud, great and rich
Yes, they go far to ridicule and belittle.

O yes, I wish they knew their end
See them, pitiable fellows
But here they are judging others.

THE CONFUSION

I pity men, yes I do
Men who know not their wives
Men whose concubines are uncountable
Men who cannot number their children,
Those whose children are strangers
Children with diverse blood
Born by brothers, nephews, friends, in-laws, foreigners and aliens.

Such houses filled with mixed blood
Where illegitimacy trends and thrives
An artillery of waywardness.

It baffles me a lot
In fact, I cannot envisage properly
How hooligans rule the day
How they earn respect and the people tremble.

Breeds of multiple blood
Untrained, unlearned, uncivilized and uncultured,
Together with their brand, they destroy
They destroy brands and trademarks,
Unique trademarks that are branded and outstanding.

MESSAGE

Take this message to the sky
Tell the heavens of it
That I am in desperate need of answers
I am wondering why vagabonds terrorize homes
They sell lands, properties and family belongings
They make away with anything in their care
Be it theirs or not.

This crop of family members brings shame
 They bring bad name to others and the entire family.

They care not whose ox is gored
They manipulate and manoeuvre
They lie, consciously, maliciously, dubiously
Anxiously, jealously, enviously, zealously and suspiciously,
There is nothing they cannot do or will not do,
Not do, in fact, they do everything.

Their lifestyle is a forbidden horror
They engage in all forms of sexual satisfaction,
Womanizing is only a pinch.

I am amazed at the world
We live in, what is going on and where we would arrive at.

EVIL

Domestic violence is a way of life
Exploitation is a culture
Humiliation is a tradition
Greed, selfishness, laziness and cheating are normal platforms.

Tell me why these people enjoy hurting others
The gain in pulling others down
The joy in setting others up,
The glory in reducing others
The pride in character assassination
The peace in rumour mongering
And the sense in denting others.

For all I know, and the more I care to know
I am yet to be convinced
Convinced on why people go from place to place
Bent, seriously bent on deforming,
Defaming and defaming people
Especially people of great reputation.

PAYBACK

Those who groom their children
Derive pleasure from them
Rich or poor, dead or alive
Great or small, up or down
They live fulfilled no matter what.

Those who train their children
Suffer a whole lot
But they like what they are doing
Because the future counts
A day of reckoning;
The payday.

Therefore those who do not train theirs
Should refrain from hate and jealousy
However, anybody can train anybody
One can train oneself too
So if parents or guardians fail
We can bear the load of training,
For there is a day for payback
When all works shall come to light.

Heed, we must
This life of cumbersome worry
This hustle of horrible tale
This service of endless pain,
Let us learn to weed greed and selfishness.

HEARTBREAKING

Please help me comprehend
How a husband sends away his wife
Together with his baby
Never contributes to their upkeep
But at the end he reaps.

When she is about to get married
Yes, at the wedding day
He precides as her father
And enjoys the fruits thereof.

He becomes a grandfather
Being sustained by those he rejected
Let someone help me understand
Please put me through,
Because this is heartbreaking
A culture, rugged and rural.

This culture you adore and magnify
This tradition you uphold and fertilize
I do not know how to accept it
My spirit battles with it.

Wake me up when you find answers
Suitable answers that would convince me
Reasonable and godly, humane and real
Let them bring lasting solutions
Because it is heartbreaking.

FOOLISHNESS

Tell me in crystal form
How a kindred writer loses it
How he loses the book of records,
Records of family meetings.

No fire, no flood, no theft
No travel, no transit,
Tell me the mystery of foolishness.

Do people steal things in their custody
Do they sell them
Who sells public gold,
Who buries general treasure
Do people burn kindred shrine?

Wise men do not joke with wiser men
Wiser men joke not with wisdom
Lest they all be made fools and foolish.

Let them know that quiet people are tamed
They raise alarm too,
They blow up places when they wish
They trumpet at will
Yes, their alarm and whistle are deadlier
They raise dust, dusty dust that cannot be dusted,
It is not foolishness.

Witch hunting and clamours
 Gangups and cliques
Portable and culpable majority;
All, foolish and fullness of foolishness.

MADNESS

Now, I want to know why
A timid widow whose husband is yet unburied
Will fight a relative,
One who came to see how they are faring
Who was actually compelled by another as escort.

A rude widow, wayward and uncultured
Whose livelihood depends on others
Others whom she dares not ridicule.

She has no control, no boundary
She fights and barks like a dog
Her courage, audacity and background yet pale.

I have said this before
Now, I repeat it
The world is bleeding
Yes, this globe is giving up
I guess, it is time.

CRAZINESS

A weird story
Scandal and rumour
Character assassination,
Just to humiliate and darken.

How a charm tied in a stick
Penetrates a bathing woman
In dream, real life or imagination
Wonders shall never end.

She says it, she sings it
The reason she is barren
Craziness in the highest order
Whoever believes is crazier than her.

People rest their frustrations on others
They cook evil stories to support them
They convince the gullible
And gather their likes
They bear grudge and hate
They keep malice together and on their behalf.

But someday, they shall account
Yes, according to their false accusations
All the muddy waters they poured on others.

And this is for them all
When the time comes,
Let them never cry foul!

GREED

They say they are freedom fighters
They are an umbrella
An umbrella under a religion
Yet, they do horrors.

They buy lands everywhere
They grab as many as possible
They buy from wrong people
Who claim ownership,
They go to court and fight dirty
They intimidate whoever they can.

No due process, short time, short notice
They exchange freedom for bondage
They bind sellers in heavy chains
Chains of perpetual slavery and ignorance,
Yet they say they serve God.

Which heaven ordains that prophet
And which God sends that Messiah?
Answer me.

Do churches banish members who refuse selling their lot
Do churches force people to sell their inheritance?

This mission is greed
Hate is their missionary
My heart bleeds
Yes, I am troubled
Because evil has overtaken good
And the world is comfortable.

GREEDINESS

When people who labour selflessly
And work tirelessly,
When people serve meritoriously and diligently
When people show honesty and loyalty
When they exhibit passion and humanity
When they display integrity and wisdom
When they put in their best even at danger,
Why won't they be rewarded?

Sound men of high intelligence
Great heroes of radiant valour
Radical comrades of pure service
Service per excellence
Men who fought for restoration
Restoration of peace and order,
Giants that instilled discipline
Yet, they are dead and forgotten.

Which sane land and clime does so?
Treating veterans with utmost disdain
I am troubled by selfishness
I am ashamed of ungodliness
Because they have ruined our land.

It pains my heart
Yes, it does, that men honour money
They respect those who disobey them
They crown and enthrone them
But disregard those who do all for them
Those who put their lives on the line serving them.

People take advantage of them
They use and abuse them
Those who sincerely fight for them
They believe those people are ordinary
Easy to come by, and fools.

Tell them that a pinch on loyalty brings tumour
A stain on respect breeds cancer, and cankerworms
The one that cannot easily be cured,
Tell them, paying good with evil is unimaginable.

KARMA

When people wish you madness
And it strikes them
When they wish you bastards
And lo, bear them
When they wish you evil
And, they see it
Tell me how you feel.

Feel it, anyhow you want it
There is God that answers prayers
It depends on how and when He chooses.

I may not forget how it looks
How it feels, or the rage it tears
But sure, I know how it feels
When scandalized, gossipped, ridiculed
Mocked, laughed at, slandered
I tell you, I know, I really do.

There is karma
The other is nemesis
Repercussion is a mother
It bears children
It is never barren.

PAIN

When people wake up with boxing hand against you
When they draw the battle line
When they announce your defeat
And celebrate your death,
Do you still pray or believe in God?

The heart that bleeds knows more pain
Yes, it knows more than the eyes that cry,
A weeping soul has no sleep
For the night is long and far,
Sleep is gone, rest is dead
That is how it is when men fight you
When they want you gone and forgotten,
When they vow to weed you off the earth.

However, there is a time of appointment
A time given to both the strong and the weak
The living and the dead,
The born and the unborn
Yes, this time is predestined
It is the true announcer.

Forget the show, the noise of the battle
Victory is not the music
Victory is the conquest,
Armours and weapons lose wars
The almighty warrior does not,
The pain shall be killed
The painmaker shall be ashamed
When victory arrives, pain shall be gone.

I NEED ANSWERS

Why do leaders forget their followers
Why does the head play with the neck that bears it
Why does the body suffer the legs that walk it,
Why are they so ignorant of their needs and duties?

They function separately
They live independently
They discriminate and segregate against each other
Fools, thinking life revolves around them, why?

Followers die in silence
Models showcase nonsense,
Guardians forget their responsibilities
Mentors deceive
Why, why, who knows?

A child uses his parent for ritual
A brother donates his sister
An aunt sacrifices her niece
An uncle sells his nephew
Rituals, quests, urge upon urge
Lust, greed, hate, disunity, bitterness
Why, why, when will it end?

People no longer tell the truth
What do they gain from fraud and fraudulent deals?

Some deceive women and ladies
Just to sleep with them
Some behave real to manoeuvre
Just for awhile
Only to get satisfied per minute.

RELIGIOUS MADNESS

The latest are prophets and seers
They prophesy and see visions
Nothing but evil.

They can never predict good
They cook bad stories
Just to dupe ignorant and desperate people.

They sow discord in homes and families
Relationships and businesses
Because they need nothing but money.

Tell me why evil has gained so much ground
That crowds follow suit,
We have accepted to live with it happily
Some have become norms.

Prophets, fake prophets and unreal seers
They perform horrors to get power
Powers destroying lives.

They have ruined directly
They have abused indirectly
They never came from God
Prophets of Baal roaming, roaring, killing.

Tell me why it is so
Why must we keep being victims
Are we not fools or have we not been fooled enough?

Wake up, rise up, face the fact
Hungry wolves are ruining the temple of God
They are magicians
They are morticians
Dirty and filty
Blaspheming God, mocking Him.

STIGMATIZATION

Infertility is a disease
But some are curable,
Whether in men or in women
It is not gender-based
Barrenness can be anybody's fault
Why suspect or accuse women only?

Let us help sick people
Victims of any kind can be saved
We should not victimize victims
Discrimination kills, some suicides boil down to such.

Bullying is a crime
Love can heal
Kindness is great
Cheerfulness can save
Save the world.

Enough of these stigmatization
The world is vast
Large and complex, enough for all of us.

ARROGANCE

Rich people show off their wealth
Riches acquired and amassed rightly, wrongly
Especially when they see poor people
Those that they can intimidate,
They force them to worship them
Because life was not fair enough.

Tell me why it should be so
This bleeding heart wails, weeps
Trying to find answers, answers that bewilder
Answers that only God knows where they are.

Rich people display money
Useless and needless money,
They make a mess of it, with it, for it and around it
While poor people are everywhere begging for bread.

They prefer being worshipped and served
They want these poor folks to be perpetually redundant
So I ask why can't people help others
Mostly green stars?

IGNORANCE

When some people take ill
They suspect some people,
They would not go to see a doctor
They run to prayer houses,
They suspect people especially relatives, colleagues
Evil spirit, bad dreams, and strange thoughts
They recall omens, good and bad
Whatever be their sickness,
It baffles me that even educated people do same.

Even when karma comes
When nemesis traces them
When repercussion knocks
When compensation whispers
When consequences arrive,
We still have the guts to suspect who is killing us.

Of all the ugly thing we do
Of all terrible altars we bowed at
Shrines and idols
We run to prophets to prophesy
To name our killers, doers and poisoners
Or whoever, some fake seers to see.

We forget that life is neither smooth nor rosy
Not even straight, not even cool
We fly, we run, we fall, we slip off, we sleep
We lose, we gain, we cry, we laugh, we move
We need, we want, we lack, we thirst, we hunger
We win, we do all these and more
And things happen how they were ordained.

INEQUALITY

Some people have special children
Children who nature chose,
They treat them badly.

They hide them
They wish them death
But cater for others well
Because they are normal.

Why hide them, why maltreat them
When they should receive more time and love?
No doubts, it is burdensome and challenging
But then, they are humans
With flesh and blood in veins,
They are gifted too
Their gifts can be harnessed rightly
Then the world would appreciate heavens.

Special children bear the brunt of negligence
Loneliness and boredom are their companion,
Sometimes they attempt suicide if chance be
Let us love them better and harder
Let us attend to them properly,
They never chose to be so.

Children generally require special care
They can only become responsible when pruned
We should not abuse them nor misuse them
We have to nurture and educate them
Train, harness, welcome and enjoy them.

DENIAL

When you strike a deal with people
Especially deal involving money they deny
They alter, default, frustrate, misread, misreport the evidence.

Some go as far as killing, indicting
Some destroy all evidences
Some disappear, some accuse you of stealing,
Woe betide you if nothing was ever recorded
Totally gone, you dare not raise the topic
Because you would lose generally,
Your name, your deal, your respect, everything
The pain, regret, loss, anger and burden
All rest on your head.

Smart people think they are truly smart
Clever ones hail themselves great
They forget spiritual witnesses
Kindred spirits and terrestrial spirits
They think they have fooled you alone.

Why is money the central point of all things today
Why has it become a god that people worship dearly
Why are people losing everything in place of money?

I am yet to find out why money governs all
Why it commands such influence,
More influential than love, truth, unity, and peace.

GANG

They form groups
In rows, columns, centers
They live in holes
Holes that make them whole
Why? Because they have set their traps.

Traps to catch the innocent
The mild, meek, gentle and poor
The ones whose voices are not strong
Those whose strengths are low
The ones they place no value on
They gather to hurt and ruin them.

These gatherers and gangs think they are God
They see less than tomorrow
They brag how mighty they are
But actually they are blind.

Blind, because anything can happen
Of a truth, the counsel of the wicked shall not stand
They gather in lustful vain and vanity
They gang in error
Their strength and voice fail
Because there is God.

THE SECRET

Hear the secret of peace
Where there is trouble
Peace cannot live.

Trouble troubles those that trouble him
Peace does not trouble trouble.

Look away from disaster
The ones we plant
The ones they plant
The ones we harvest
The ones we enjoy
And all forms of trouble
For only then shall we have peace.

When we spread hate
And speak hatefully
We poison minds and souls
We murder spirits and abuse hearts
These poisonings trouble the land
And the land hurts our feet
Our feet that run helter skelter.

Be careful, watch, pray, wait, hope
This hate we plant only ruins
Nothing good it brings
Tomorrow is a mystery
Mysterious people understand only but a few.

BLEEDING HEART

These troubles ache my heart
They make me cry and weep
Many nights I think
I ponder and wonder
And my spirit wanders
Trying to find reasons and answers
Why communities clash.

They fight, war and battle
They drag material things
Things that are never worth their blood.

Why can't peace rule
Why can't unity echo
Why can't humans understand themselves?
Fightings, killings, clashes, wars
How long shall we live like this?

Young people wanting to die
Allowing themselves to be used wrongly
Old ones ignoring their responsibilities
People igniting troubles
Fomenting chokes
Rekindling hate
Communal clashes claiming vibrant lives.

PERSONAL INTERESTS

Greedy people inciting trouble
Selfish groups instigating hate
Insignificant few, portable fellows
Craving for autonomy.

They go extra miles
They build ropes and ladders
They block bridges and connections
They stand like vampires
Ready to suck, not to be suckled.

Autonomy everywhere, here and there
Wishes, drives, campaigns, indoctrinations
Wrong and childish imbibing
Personal interests, selfish gains
Family quests, greed and greediness
Yearnings of improper and untimely dreams
Dubious channels and mischievous canals,
That keeps me wondering
Where are we heading to?

Must money and pride fight others
Must pomposity and arrogance bully
Must these people teach vain things,
Can't they upgrade generally instead of wars
Fighting wrong courses that harbour curses?

TIMES

Initially, it was by merit
Everything was earned
Respect, dignity, pride and purity
But no longer today.

Today, respect is bought by the rich
Dignity is sought by the rude
Honour is given to the silly
Pride crowns the rogue,
Nothing is ever great again.

Grades, certificates, positions
Appointments, assignments, contracts
Nothing seems real anymore.

School and education were twins
Inseparable, unbeatable, unconquerable
Credentials were real, merited, valid and unique
Today, they appear to be mere papers
Papers without much value
My heart bleeds
Because times have changed.

Fools pranking the wise
Cowards tricking the brave
Minors cheating the majors
In fact, I cannot understand times anymore.

Who made it so
Why is it so
What caused it so
Because in the beginning
It was not so?

CROOKS

Lands in the rural areas are bread
They are gold and diamond
In a sense so unbelievable.

Collective lands become treasures
Treasures that some can corner them
Corner and do away with in their own way.

Land sharing in families become mockery
A challenge that can lead to court
Some individuals wanting more
Others getting much
Some deserving less
Others demanding all.

Family inheritance
Kindred portions
Communal lands,
Greedy fellows cooking methods
Seeking avenues to sell up or own all
Selfish folks fronting strangers
Organizing cruel and silly patterns
Tactics of ungodly chain
Luring themselves to lord all.

These compound my confusion
Why people are greedy and selfish
Why they kill to gain everything,
Why they manipulate others to feed
Why their stomach is never filled,
They make me wonder in wonder.

DOWRY

Confused still and worried more
I still search for answers
Why do people demand for towers
Towers of items for marriage ceremony?

In some parts of the world
People almost sell their daughters
In the name of marriage,
They frustrate grooms and in-laws
In the guise of marriage rites.

Why is it so
Must it be so,
If they regain everything spent on her training
Would they never accept anything from the in-laws?

Why would people suffer, murmur and cry
While performing marriage rites?
Can't all these be minimal and minimized,
And some totally abolished?

Does high bride price place high value, dignity,
Integrity, trust, love on the bride?

Some perform rituals so crazy
Some flog, some fight, some starve
Some harm and starve themselves
Some bleed and wound their bodies
Just to prove love, readiness, strength,
Why are these cultures still in existence?

MOURNING

In some parts of the world
When people die
Relatives wail and mourn
They mourn deeper
They do so because of the burden of burial rites.

Relatives, in-laws, maternal homes, kindreds
Villages, clans, communities, societies, groups,
Traditional and religious, all must be settled,
Sometimes these groups barely help in the rites.

Why would people be so mean in making rules
Regulations, stipulations and constitutions,
Why would they force and compel people to dry up
Stripping them of money, strength and hope
All in the name of burial?

When the rich die, it becomes a celebration
Competitions of unnecessary ends
Introductions of crazy ceremonies,
When the poor die,
They mourn their dead terribly alone in pains.

Why are burial ceremonies becoming tournaments?
Some groups stay for days being fed by the bereaved,
Some act nonsense dramas hurting deeper the grieving,
Cultures so weird and whacky,
It baffles me, it astonishes me
And I keep wondering.

POLYGAMOUS FAMILY

Polygamous families are great
They number and outnumber many
They teem and team up
For or against others
But many a time, they are a wrestling ring.

Why do they become boundless and numberless
That sometimes, one barely knows them all?
They scatter across and wherever
Some become a republic
That they force themselves on other family members,
Even when they cannot because they are unsound.

But in the olden days
People enjoyed polygamous families
Especially children from such homes,
Because they had large barns, farms and lands
Palm trees, breadfruits, livestock and other agricultural produce.

Today, why are there more troubles in such homes,
Is it education, illiteracy, disunity, hate and envy
Jealousy, intruders or spiritual fate?

NEW SCHOOL

Young people today do drugs
They drink, smoke, womanize, and tout
They do whatever they feel like
With little or no thought about the consequences.

Some choose between schooling and touting
They hate discipline, control and morals
They want freedom, freedom at all cost.

In fact they have debased laws, norms
Traditions and cultures, they have mutilated,
So cultureless, a generation
New school with everything absurd.

My heart bleeds for them, yes
I cannot foresee the future,
If the present is frightening and this ungodly
Won't the future be a terrible hell?

Tell me why the youths should be wayward
Lawlessly proud and arrogant,
Immoral, untamed, uncultured, unrepentant
And willing to die.

My heart bleeds for this new school
A generation so godless and fearless
Blunt, yet timid
Exposed yet outdated
Obsolete yet up to date,
Who can save the youth,
Can't you see a generation futurelessly crazy?

JUNGLE JUSTICE

Stealing is of many types
And each is wrong
Requiring different punishments,
However, it is horrible
How many behave toward thieves.

Jungle justice is evil
It is a crime itself
When people catch a suspect or thief
They naked them
Beat them up,
And even set some ablaze.

Meanwhile there are bigger thieves
Unseen, unheard, unknown, uncaught
 Thieves who steal large, and larger treasures
Treasuries and destinies of nations
They steal lives and futures
People consciously and unconsciously worship them.

We must refrain from jungle justice
These groups of people or thieves burnt
May even be innocent,
But people rarely give them time to talk
Explain or prove themselves,
Some mobs harden their hearts
No answer, no explanations convince them
They are totally bent on killing victims.

My heart bleeds, it really does
People who are killed over nothing
Flimsy excuses and reasons,
Even a suspect is innocent until proven guilty by the law.

How we lost humanity still baffles me
How we became so wicked and heartless
That we set fellow humans on fire
Taking pictures and making videos of them burning,
I still wonder who brought us here.

TRESPASS

Again, I cannot understand
Why people encroach into lands
Lands that are not theirs.

Why they trespass and intrude
Some gradually do
Some instantly do
Some automatically do
Some forcefully do
Some do it anyhow, anytime
That wonders me a lot.

People intentionally take what is not theirs
They manufacture proofs to back themselves up
They involve lots of horrible means,
A world so immoral.

Why won't my heart bleed
When people prefer malicious dealings
To gracious enterprises?

They sell other people's lands and inheritance
They sell same property to several people
They gather men to fight
They disappear for awhile
And return later to continue.

I need answers and reasons
I want to be convinced
Convinced on why people sell one property many times
To many people.

What is their gain, joy and pride
What is their happiness and duty towards man,
I wonder, and wonder and wonder
Yes, this wonderment is afar off seeking answers.

DECEIT

When men put ladies in marriage way
With no intention of marrying them,
I get confused.

Some cohabit, bearing children
They convince them that they are their partners
They make these women believe in them
They play them like musical instruments.

Why do men hurt women this far
After the time, energy, love, lust
Sweat, emotions, dreams, and contributions,
Why would a sane man do so?

Why do we fight for nature
Only to fight against it actually,
We truncate time and push it backward
We stop chances and lucks
We fold and foil destinies
Especially the ones that are meant to be.

As you preserve yourself
So preserve another
Let he who loves love not give hate
For whatever you give, you will receive.

We have turned the world upside down
My heart wonders and wanders
Wondering and pondering,
A wanderer in Wonder.

INTRUDERS

In a family, group, kindred, society
People with ulterior motives intrude
They divide them into visible and invisible sections
In order to gain their way.

These groups work together to thwart their efforts
Or against in order to achieve their selfish goal.

Many a time, could be fools
Illiterates and cowards,
They use this medium to infiltrate
And scatter a unified body with force.

Sometimes, inferiority complex contributes
And so do discrimination and segregation.

However, a wise man takes counsel
Not to heed to a fool, no matter what,
Despite their numbers because a foolish majority offers nothing.
All get confused why they love divisions and pollutions.

ABUSE

The genital mutilation is archaic
It could be infectious too,
Why go through such a crude practice?

We must learn to drop ugly cultures
That mar womanhood and mankind.

Old traditions that are indecent and ungodly
The ones, cruel, barbaric, atrocitic and painful
Some of these are abuses that must stop.

Flogging men to know their strength
Beating and marking women to determine their endurance
Trust, faithfulness, ability, and level of love
In some areas and lands,
Some parts of the world
That are still timid and primitive
These and other weird cultures must be abolished.

My heart bleeds for these terrible acts
Especially acts against women, children
The female gender,
Many people see women as second class
Inferior colleagues, sex objects
Toys and beauty furniture.

This is so inhumane and must be stopped
I cannot understand
 What makes them feel better
Stronger, and superior
When they hurt, harm and torment vulnerable people.

CURIOSITY

I want to know more of people
Their characters, habits, goals, aims
Objectives, motives, actions and reasons
Especially behind some of their behaviours.

I am curious to find out
Why are people unreliable
Unrealistic, unstable, unsteady
Untrue, unfaithful, disrespectful?

They cannot stand by their words
They change with the weather
They follow the trend
They enjoy the bandwagon
They just care not about the outcome.

Why are people so cunning
They convince you to follow them
They swear they are with you
Beside you, for you, around you
But lo and behold
All is nothing but deceit.

Except you are willing or ignorant to die for them
You are just on you own, why?
I am very curious to know why
Who is ready to feed me answers?

TRICKS

On the feast day
Everyone is present,
On the fight day
They are absent,
Leaving it to the warriors
Warriors they disregard.

They gather and merry
They eat and dance
They celebrate and enjoy
Because the occasion is joyful.

But the day for decision
The day to wrestle and struggle
The day to help others
The day to tell the truth
The day to call a spade a spade
Tom would disappear
Dick would travel,
Harry would fall sick,
Tricks and pranks
Tactics and diplomacy
Calculated and targeted at selfish interest.

Incredible humans, unscrupulous elements
Dancing in the rain to entice children
But they run from responsibilities,
The real issues of life.

I wonder how these tricks help
How they build nations
How they save generations
How they welcome the future,
I keep wondering.

SOCIETY

Why do boys normally get away
Yes, they get away from certain wrongs
When they impregnate a girl
They flee, then the girl suffers
She goes through traumas and dramas
Sometimes alone, sometimes rejected,
Sometimes dejected, depressed, abandoned.

But the boys go on
They move as if nothing happened
In the future, they come claiming paternity,
Especially when the child becomes something great
Or when they need him to sustain their lineage.

Sometimes, I wonder why the world is this harsh
Why women suffer hell
Even when they bring and nurture life.

HATRED

Some people hate others
Even at the point of blocking their progress,
They envy, antagonize, attack them openly and secretly.

Some others hide theirs only to harm them later
Yet they openly pretend to love them
They claim to cherish and care for them.

This hate goes as far as gathering others to hate them too
Either by castigating them, gossiping or denting their image
They also force people to love those they love,
They tend to manipulate all in their favour.

It gets me troubled
When people stop others from getting married
When they doublecross would-be-in-laws
Especially painting spinsters evil to suitors.

I wonder the joy they derive
From destroying people's hope and future,
Backbiting, betrayal and ungodly movements.

They stop marriage proposals
They stop job opportunities
They steal contracts
They connive with others to dupe their friends
They pretend to be friendly
But they are evil, why?

CHANGE

The youths are the leaders of tomorrow
Yes, I agree, I hope so too
They are the backbone of every society
And the future generations,
But it worries me why many are towing wrong path.

Becoming vagabonds, drug addicts, criminals
Dropouts, touts, disrespectful, disobedient, untamed,
Clubbing and partying
Drinking and betting,
Hoping to become millionaires and billionaires
In a twinkle, just like that, without labour.
This disturbs my peace.

It is hard to believe the chances
Yes, the possibility of having good homes with these
The future is scary, because the youths are becoming crazy.

If I tell you, I worry not
I am a big liar,
A wonderment, I cannot imagine.

FAST LANE

No one labours sincerely anymore
No one wants to be diligent again
No one wishes to suffer before pleasure
Everyone wants to follow the fast lane.

This fast lane weakens my heart
It splits my thoughts in hundreds
And scatters my understanding.

How can one grow overnight,
How can one become a giant from cradle?

People build mansions and skyscrapers
They live in palaces and kingdoms
Being kings and queens
Without foundations.
I wonder why and how
How and why, I keep wondering.

I fear the future
The future fears me,
The future I fear is frightening
The world is pregnant
And her pregnancy is haunting.

Will she deliver stillbirth
Will it be a stillborn,
Is it likely to be premature?
I wonder, my spirit wonders.

BEHIND THE SCENE

People pretend to be in love
When they are actually incompatible,
They try to hide scars
Scars that are shiny and obvious.

They form good when on surveillance
But they are really demons when unwatched.

When people die, we spend money
We give them befitting burial,
We buy golden casket and diamond suit
We hire mourners and undertakers
Unfortunately, these people starved to death.

They were naked, they were lonely
They were forgotten and unloved
No one ever cared for them,
They were jobless, they were helpless and hopeless
We could have helped, but we never did.

They were sick, lame, blind, deaf and dumb
They were talented and gifted
We were supposed to push them up
To give a helping hand,
But we intentionally ignored them
We pretentiously allowed them to suffer
To taste hell on earth,
But when they die, we release cash
We hire bands, we bring various performers
We fly friends from different corners of the world
Just to pay them last respect,
People whom we actually neglected to die.

Wickedness in the highest order
Pretense, ungodliness, lack of love.

Behind the scene, we nailed them
Behind the scene, we abandoned them
Behind the scene, we hated them
Behind the scene, we actually killed them.

PAMPERING

Rich children win the hearts of their parents
They gain their prayers and blessings
They gather good names from them
And favour because they are rich, why?

Why do people gamble with family
Why do they separate and segregate because of wealth,
They place rich and richer ones higher
And give poor ones no regards, why?

They pamper wealthy children
And disperse poor ones,
Children from the same womb
Is it ignorance, hate or selfishness,
Is it materialism or just nature?

Does anyone give blessings
Does anyone give life or death,
Who gives manna
Who waters the desert,
Why do some parents divide their homes
Because of perishable wealth?

Life is decayable
Wealth is vanishable
But name, good name, goodwill always last.

Families, colleagues, friends and people
Humans give unequal respect to others
Because of fame, money, position
Pampering wrongly, destroying relationship
Cautiously, consciously and otherwise.

Please be humble
Treat people right
Tomorrow is a mystery
Only God enthrones or dethrones.

SIDE CHICKS

I do not know what side chicks want
I doubt if they want true life at all,
What are their dreams
Do they have ambitions, hopes and aspirations?
They make me wonder and ponder.

Is life actually about sleeping with men
Changing beds and rooms and men
Especially with married men?

Where is the sense in it
Scattering homes, shattering families
Tormenting children, ruining lives?

Does life remain static
Is life rewindable
That they choose to be so useless?

Flashing irrelevant and material things as goals
Endangering themselves to get trendy wears
Contracting diseases, transmitting same
Blinding themselves and living in bondage
Would all these keep them in Paradise?

I wonder what would be their teachings
Their lessons and legacies
Especially when they luckily or finally settle down,
What their children in particular would happily hear.

FORGERY

The brain is the storehouse
It is there to store our dealings
Our memory is incredible
It gives us what we give it, and more.

Certificates bought or forged
Degrees stolen or sold
None can be defended.

We know our abilities and capabilities
For those who buy or sell,
For those who upgrade papers not head
For those who buy promotions
Papers are not brains,
And they can never be.

The door is legal
The window is theft
The door is real
The ceiling is outrageous
Wherever we enter from
The realities are obvious,
And the legalities are outstanding.

RESPONSIBILITIES

Tell the married men who know not
That tomorrow is pregnant,
Tell them to come home
Go home and be home,
Tell them to train their children
Tell them that irresponsibleness is not a medal
And no one boldly wears them.

Let them know that home is good
Home is God,
Home is life
Home is peace,
Home is love
Home is wealth,
Let them know that they are there to fix it.

Tell parents that society depends on nurturing
They should not be careless and wayward,
Train your children, discipline them
Culture and tame them
Otherwise you live in nightmares.

A man is God
There are expectations from him
Let them Mann their homes
Tell them to fill the loopholes they create
Until then, there is trouble.

Tell them that life is bit by bit, phase by phase
Stage by stage, time by time, turn by turn
Married people, especially men, build your homes
Stop running away from responsibilities
You may not be perfect
But you must be a human.

BOUNDARY

I want to know why great preachers do not visit the poor
Why they do not attend their funerals and ceremonies,
Why do they attend funerals of only the rich
And associate only with them?

They wed their children
They officiate their burials
They open and bless their houses
They dedicate their cars
They baptize their families
And hang around rich and influential people.

Why do they marry themselves
And their children find life easier,
Why do men of God wake up the rich
And pray for them,
But never step their feet on the poor's home?

Does the poor not need God
Do they not need these men of God,
Do they not have houses, homes and gifts
Are they lepers and outcasts
Are they unclean, uncircumcised and unholy?

Do the poor chase away the holy spirit
Don't they give offerings in the church,
Do they not adhere to doctrines and rules
How did they offend the ministers of God?

I keep wondering
It marvels me
It baffles me
It remains a wonderment to me.

BIRDS OF SAME FEATHER

Why do people cover evil
Why do they harbour it,
That it hatches?

What good is in it
That sustains it,
What flavour is it
That retains it,
I mean, why do they hate truth
And the speakers of truth
Why do they also love the doers of iniquity?

Imperfect beings can be clean
Feeble minds can be holy
Tender ones can be great
If and only if they care to.

Humans are imperfect
But they can be blessed,
Men are not God
But they are the image of God,
Hence they resemble Him.

WONDERMENT

Why do people love lies
And garnish hate,
Why do they paint white black
And black, white?

Why lying against innocent people
Why slandering innocent ladies,
You say they aborted
You lie that they had children out of wedlock
You say they sold their babies
You lie they hid them in strange lands,
Why scandalizing pure brides?

Virginity reigns, it does
Take it, leave it
Cleanness is real
Virtue, patience, morals, godliness
All and their likes still stand
No one can take them away.

PURITY

No matter how dark, they paint
No matter, how mean they are
No matter how evil they portray
No matter how wide they spread,
Purity is a god,
It fights for those who keep it.

Go ahead, lie and lie
Keep scandalizing and slandering
Dear champion of gossip
You warrior of treachery
You son of lust and greed
Your cup will soon run over.

Black tongue of debasing calling
Loose lips of fetish oiling
Tight arms of uneven yoke
Your flag is dark, high above the sky
Flying like an aeroplane
Transporting people in inhumane realms,
Your day is coming
Yes, in full force
Because purity is unquestionable.

Yes, purity is stainless
Nothing can reduce it,
Forces testify
Men can only obey.

NGOZI OLIVIA OSUOHA is a poet, writer, thinker, she is a graduate of Estate Management with experience in Banking and Broadcasting. She has published fourteen books and has also featured in over sixty international anthologies, she equally has published over two hundred and fifty poems in over twenty countries. Some of her poems have been translated and published into Russian, Romanian, Spanish, Arabic, Farsi, Polish, Khloe, and other languages. She has numerous words on marble. She has won several awards and she's one time BEST OF THE NET NOMINEE.

www.ingramcontent.com/pod-product-compliance
Lightning Source LLC
Chambersburg PA
CBHW071749040426
42446CB00012B/2505